QUEEN ELIZABETH I

PAPER DOLLS TO CUT OUT AND COLOR

with text by
Queen Elizabeth I
herself
about her
favorites.

1596

BELLEROPHON BOOKS • 36 Anacapa Street, Santa Barbara, CA 93101

QUEEN ELIZABETH I on the front cover is by or after George Gower, c. 1588, in the National Portrait Gallery (no. 541), London. The 'Phoenix Portrait' on the back cover is attributed to Nicolas Hilliard, c. 1575, National Portrait Gallery (no. 190), London. QUEEN ELIZABETH I in the letter E on this page is from the Book of Statutes of the Plaisterers' Company, 1596, in the Guildhall Library (MS. 6132), London. Holding letter B, here, is Lord Burghley, the queen's great treasurer; from an engraving by Franciscus Hogenberg, 1568.

The Trouble With Mary Queen of Scots

by Queen Elizabeth I

She is the person by whom our Kingdom and Crown was challenged almost as soon as Almighty God called us by right thereunto. How many ways that challenge was furthered needeth not to be recited. Remember the things done by the Scottish Queen after the death of her husband King Francis; we requested her, according to a certain Treaty of Peace concluded in 1560, to confirm the said Treaty; to this our request, delay was used, which was not convenient to nourish friendship, but rather engender suspicion. And when she returned into Scotland, we eftsoons sent to her, and demanded the same again, with offer of all manner of good friendship, which being again deferred upon pretences. We forbore for that time, but not without great cause of misliking. Then it chanced that a young Nobleman, our near kinsman, brought up in our Court, named the Lord Darnley, was secretly enticed to pass into Scotland and was suddenly accepted by that Queen in contract of marriage with her, as one thought to be a meet person to work troubles in our Realm for her advantage. Yea, contrary to the advice of the wiser sort of her Council, and consequently contrary to our will and liking, he was married to her in great haste.

These are glorious windy discourses.

QUEEN ELIZABETH I
From Turbevile's *Booke of Hunting*, 1575

By Wm. Rogers.

And after that it was divised to make him an instrument to work danger to us and our estate by sundry practices. When the said Queen had a Son of that marriage, we were of nature moved to set aside all occasions of unkindness, and did send thither an Ambassador to assist the christening of her Son, to whom we also were Godmother. At which time, unkindness being known to be betwixt her and her husband, although he had grievously offended us, we having compassion of the unnatural discord betwixt them, caused our said Ambassador at that time to use all the good means he could with her to repair the same, which he was not able to do. Such was become her misliking of her husband, although in him on the other side (as we heard say) was found all manner of lowliness meet for him to recover her favor.

A miserable calamity ensued shortly after to her, that the King her husband, with whom she was lately grievously offended, was cruelly strangled, and horribly murthered. The principal murtherer named the Earl Bothwell, having a virtuous lawful wife (of a great house) living, became suddenly her husband immediately upon the murther committed, who nevertheless vilely misused her, to the great grief of all her faithful subjects and friends. We were stricken with inward compassion of this her great extreme miseries and infamy, which was spread upon her, and sent to her messengers, to request her to have regard to her name and honor, and to relinquish such an odible person, being the known murtherer of her husband and an unlawful person to be married to her, and generally so evil a man in all vices, as he had the common name to excel all others in iniquity, wherein no advice of ours could prevail. But in the end being hated of all and seeking by force to subdue them that intended to prosecute the murtherer, she was forced to fly the Realm. She was in present danger to have her life taken away from her by fury of her Nation.

It followed, that when she had found means to escape to her liberty, she fell again into a second calamity as dangerous as the former; for having attempted, by force, to overcome the party that adhered to her son, who was then crowned and accepted King by the States of the Realm, her party was overthrown in her own sight, and she forced to escape by flying, with a very small number. And being hardly pursued, she was driven for safety of her life and came into England, yea, she herself dissembling her person for a time. But yet shortly after being discovered who she was, and we hearing thereof, sent forth commandment to have her comfortably and honorably used, and afterwards ordered certain persons of honor and credit to attend and wait upon her, and granted her to remain further within our Realm in a Castle of an ancient Nobleman, with all her company that escaped with her.

And thus far did things pass until this last year, in which time she again had, without our knowledge, entered into a secret dealing of marriage with a principal Nobleman of our Realm; and she by her ministers with certain of our Noblemen in the North part of our Realm burst into an open rebellion. Their meaning was chiefly to have set up her, not only in her own country, but in this our Realm. Her manner of unkind dealing against us in this dangerous sort passed over no small number of dangerous enterprises.

From a letter of Queen Elizabeth I to Sir Henry Norris, Ambassador to France, 1570. British Museum Additional Ms. 30156, slightly abridged.

Henry VII
1457-1509
Elizabeth of York
1465-1503

Arthur — Catharine[1] — Henry VIII — [2] Anne Boleyn   [3] Jane Seymour   Margaret — James IV of Scotland
1486-   of Aragon   1491-1547   1507-1536   1509-1537   1489-1541   1473-1513
1502·   1485-1536

Mary I — Philip II   Elizabeth   Edward VI   James V — Mary of Guise
1516-   of Spain   1533-1603   1537-1553   1512-1542   1515-1560
1558   1527-1598

The Relationship between Queen Elizabeth I and Mary Queen of Scots

Mary   Henry,
Queen of Scots   Lord Darnley
1542-1587   1545-1567

James VI of Scotland
and I of England
1566-1625

The Trouble With the Earl of Leicester

by Queen Elizabeth I

(The earl became Governor of the Low Countries, and the queen was furious.)

Upon a great adventure he was bound, That greatest Gloriana to him gave,

How contemptuously we conceive ourself to have been used by you, we could never have imagined, had we not seen it fall out, that a man raised up by ourself, and extraordinarily favored by us above any other subject of this land, would have in so contemptible a sort broken our commandment, in a cause that so greatly toucheth us in honor. Although you have showed yourself to make but little account, in most undutiful a sort, you may not therefore think that we have so little care as to pass so great a wrong in silence unredressed. Therefore, our express pleasure and commandment is, that all delays and excuses laid apart, you do presently, upon the duty of your allegiance, obey and fulfill what you shall be directed to do in our name. Fail you not, as you will answer the contrary at your uttermost peril. I am utterly at squares with this childish dealing.

Letter to the Earl of Leicester,
British Museum Cotton MS Galba, C. VIII, IX

From Turbevile's *Booke of Falconrie*, 1575.

Then came the Queene On prancing steede. Ballad, 1588

QUEEN ELIZABETH I AS DIANA
—from an engraving by Pieter van de Heyden, c. 1572.

Full jolly knight he seemed.

Praisd be Dianas faire and harmles light,
Praisd be the dewes, wherwith she moists the ground;
Praisd be hir beames, the glorie of the night,
Praisd be hir powre, by which all powres abound.

Sir W. Raleigh

The Trouble With Sir Walter Raleigh

From an ancient brief relation of Sir W. R.'s troubles.

When King James came into England, he found Sir Walter Raleigh (by favour of his late mistress queen Elizabeth) lord warden of the stannaries, lord lieutenant of Devonshire and Cornwall, captain of the guard, and governor of the Isle of Jersey; with a large possession of lands, both in England and Ireland. But finding him (as he said himself) a martial man, addicted to foreign affairs and great actions, he feared lest he should engage him in a war, a thing most hated, and contrary to the king's nature; whereupon he began to look upon him with a jealous eye, especially after he had presented him with a book, wherein with great animosity he opposed peace with Spain, then in treaty. He was soon accused of plotting with the Spaniard, to bring in a foreign army and proclaim the Infanta of Spain, queen of England; but without any proofs, and the thing itself as ridiculous as impossible. However, Sir Walter Raleigh was condemned without any witness brought in against him and committed prisoner to the Tower. The case was argued between a poor friendless prisoner and a king of England, and the chiefest judge was his greatest enemy.

Sir Walter Raleigh, being of vigorous constitution and perfect health, wore out sixteen years' imprisonment and had seen the disastrous end of all his greatest enemies; so that new persons now springing up in court, he found means to obtain his liberty, but upon condition to go a voyage to Guiana, in discovery of a gold mine; that unhappy voyage was betrayed from the very beginning, his designs being discovered to the Spanish ambassador. Immediately upon his return home he was made prisoner; and by the violent pursuit of the ambassador, the king resolved to take advantage of his former condemnation sixteen years past, and without any further trouble of the law, cut off his head. *I believe it was one of the greatest Masterpieces of that Ambassador to purchase* Raleigh's *head, for* Spanish *gold betrayed his life.*

A. Weldon, 1650

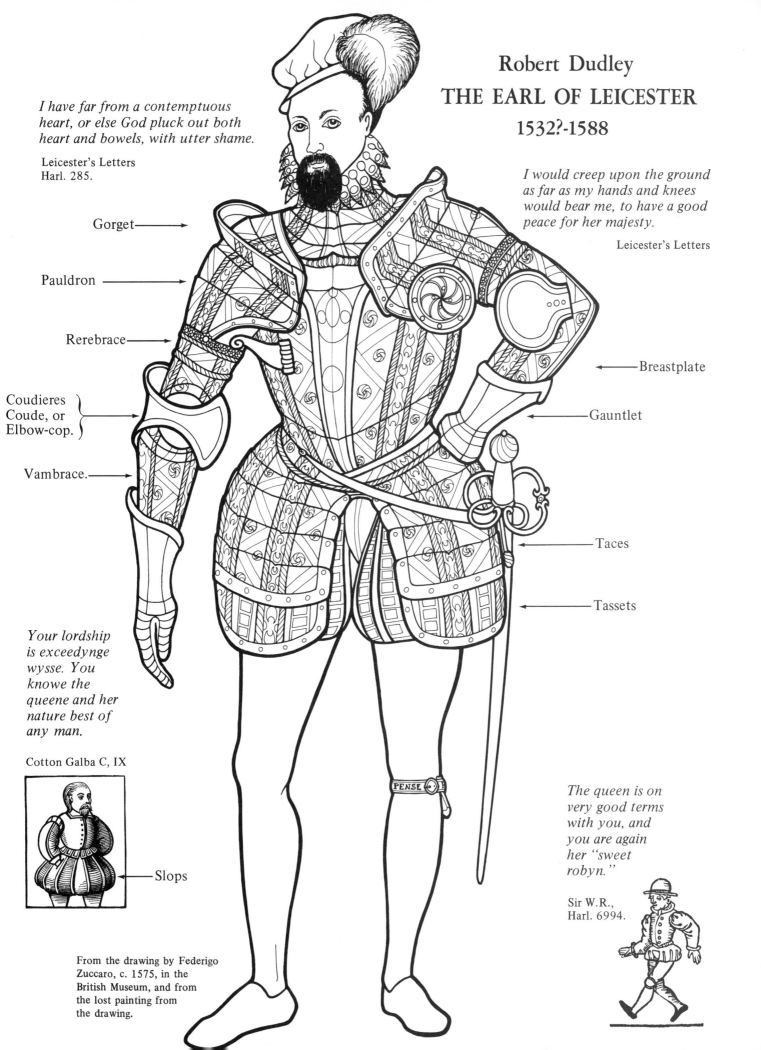

Robert Dudley
THE EARL OF LEICESTER
1532?-1588

I have far from a contemptuous heart, or else God pluck out both heart and bowels, with utter shame.

Leicester's Letters
Harl. 285.

I would creep upon the ground as far as my hands and knees would bear me, to have a good peace for her majesty.

Leicester's Letters

Gorget

Pauldron

Rerebrace

Coudieres
Coude, or
Elbow-cop.

Vambrace.

Breastplate

Gauntlet

Taces

Tassets

Your lordship is exceedynge wysse. You knowe the queene and her nature best of any man.

Cotton Galba C, IX

Slops

PENSE

The queen is on very good terms with you, and you are again her "sweet robyn."

Sir W.R.,
Harl. 6994.

From the drawing by Federigo Zuccaro, c. 1575, in the British Museum, and from the lost painting from the drawing.

THE ARMADA OF THE KING OF SPAINE
by Sir *W. Raleigh*, 1591.

From a gold rial of Queen Elizabeth I.

In the year 1588 the Spaniard purposed the invasion of England; their Navy, which they termed invincible, consisting of 240. saile of ships, not only of their own kingdom, but strengthened with the greatest Argosies, *Portugall* Caractes, Florentines and huge Hulkes of other countries; were by thirtie of her Majesties owne shippes of warre, and a few of our owne Marchants, by the wise, valiant, and most advantagious conduction of the L. *Charles Howard,* high Admirall of England, beaten and shuffeled togither; even from the Lizard in *Cornwall:* first to *Portland,* where they shamefully left *Don Pedro de Valdes,* with his mightie shippe: from *Portland* to *Cales,* where they lost *Hugo de Moncado,* with the Gallias of which he was captain, and from *Calles* driven with squibs from their anchors: were chased out of the sight of England, round about *Scotland* and *Ireland:* a great part of them were crusht against the rocks. They did not in all their sailing rounde about England, so much as sinke or take one ship of ours: or even burnt so much as one sheepcote of this land. When as on the countrarie, Syr *Francis Drake,* with only 800. souldiers not long before, landed in their Indies, and forced *Santiago, Santo Domingo, Cartagena,* and the Fortes of *Florida.*

THE ARK ROYAL ONCE CALLED THE ARK RALEIGH

was built in 1587 for Sir Walter Raleigh, but was taken over by the Crown and rechristened the Ark Royal and used as the flagship of Howard of Effingham, Lord High Admiral. The first fight with the Armada began on July 21, 1588, with the 'mighty thundering out of this ship.'

From an engraving by an unknown Elizabethian, 1588. British Museum.

HOW TO USE THE STANDS

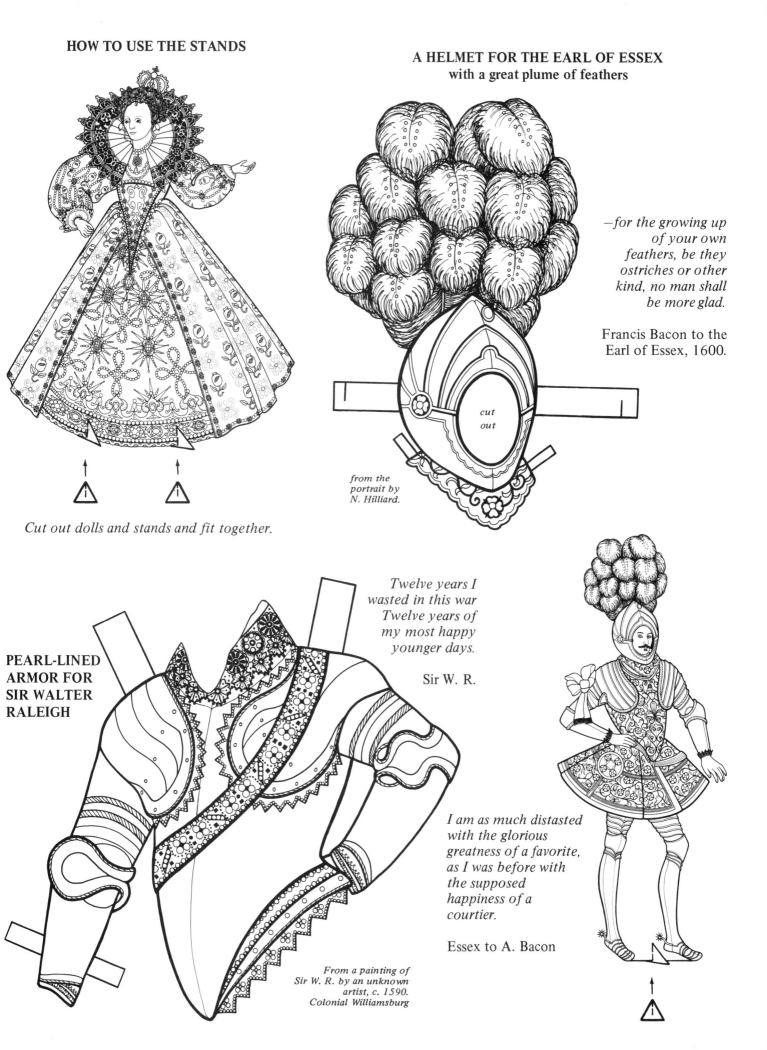

Cut out dolls and stands and fit together.

A HELMET FOR THE EARL OF ESSEX
with a great plume of feathers

cut out

from the portrait by N. Hilliard.

—for the growing up of your own feathers, be they ostriches or other kind, no man shall be more glad.

Francis Bacon to the Earl of Essex, 1600.

PEARL-LINED ARMOR FOR SIR WALTER RALEIGH

Twelve years I wasted in this war Twelve years of my most happy younger days.

Sir W. R.

I am as much distasted with the glorious greatness of a favorite, as I was before with the supposed happiness of a courtier.

Essex to A. Bacon

From a painting of Sir W. R. by an unknown artist, c. 1590. Colonial Williamsburg

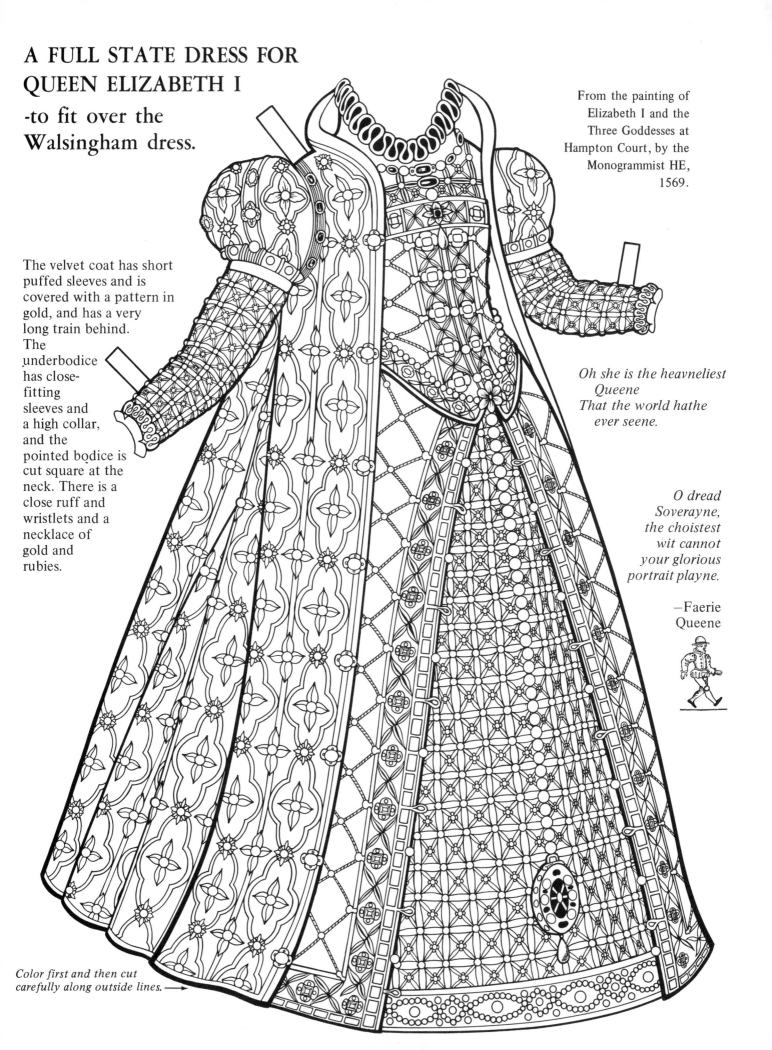

A FULL STATE DRESS FOR QUEEN ELIZABETH I

-to fit over the Walsingham dress.

From the painting of Elizabeth I and the Three Goddesses at Hampton Court, by the Monogrammist HE, 1569.

The velvet coat has short puffed sleeves and is covered with a pattern in gold, and has a very long train behind. The underbodice has close-fitting sleeves and a high collar, and the pointed bodice is cut square at the neck. There is a close ruff and wristlets and a necklace of gold and rubies.

*Oh she is the heavneliest Queene
That the world hathe ever seene.*

O dread Soverayne, the choistest wit cannot your glorious portrait playne.

—Faerie Queene

Color first and then cut carefully along outside lines. ➞

A DRESS FOR MARY QUEEN OF SCOTS

This is a hooped gown with a gauze veil stiffening into wings, from the engraving by Renold Elstrack to accompany that of James I. c. 1603.

A goodly lady clad in scarlet red.

She of death was guiltie found by right.

—Faerie Queene

Color first and then cut carefully along the outside lines. →

cut out for face

Tell Arts they have no soundness, but vary by esteeming, Tell schools they want profoundness and stand too much on seeming. If Arts and schools reply, give arts and schools the lie.

Sir W. R.

A DRESS TO FIT
ELIZABETH TRIUMPHANT

*The wallowing ocean hems her
    round about:
Whose raging floods do
    swallow up her foes,
And on the rocks their
    ships in pieces
    split.*

Geo. Peele, 1589

From a unique engraving
after Roger's *Eliza
Triumphans*;
British Museum.

*—if in living colors,
    and right hew,
Your self you
    covet to see
    pictured,
Who can it do
    more lively,
    or more true . . .*

Faerie Queene

*In Eighty Eight how
shee did fight
    Is knowne to all
    and some,
When the Spaniard
    came, her courage
    to tame,
    But had better
    have stay'd at
    home:
They came with
    Ships, fill'd full of
    Whipps,
    To have lasht her
    Princely Hide;
But she had a Drake
    made them all Quake,
    & bang'd them
    back and side.*

Ballad, 1603

*Color first and then cut
carefully along outside lines.* ⟶

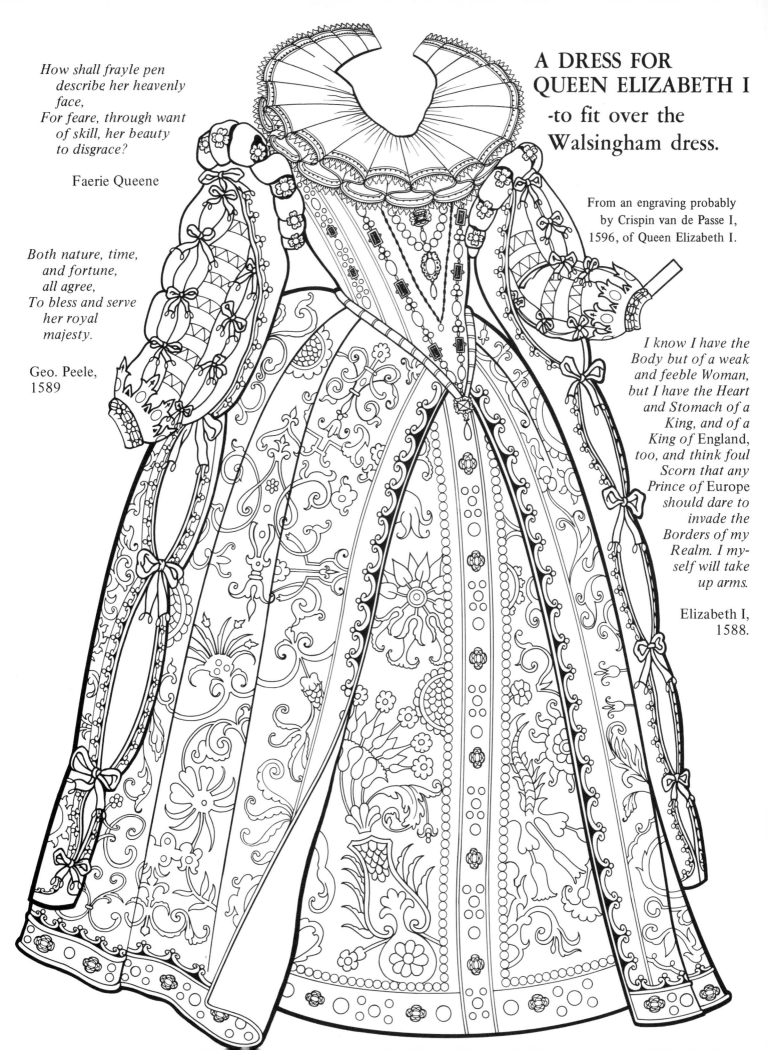

How shall frayle pen
describe her heavenly
face,
For feare, through want
of skill, her beauty
to disgrace?

Faerie Queene

Both nature, time,
and fortune,
all agree,
To bless and serve
her royal
majesty.

Geo. Peele,
1589

A DRESS FOR QUEEN ELIZABETH I
-to fit over the Walsingham dress.

From an engraving probably
by Crispin van de Passe I,
1596, of Queen Elizabeth I.

I know I have the
Body but of a weak
and feeble Woman,
but I have the Heart
and Stomach of a
King, and of a
King of England,
too, and think foul
Scorn that any
Prince of Europe
should dare to
invade the
Borders of my
Realm. I my-
self will take
up arms.

Elizabeth I,
1588.

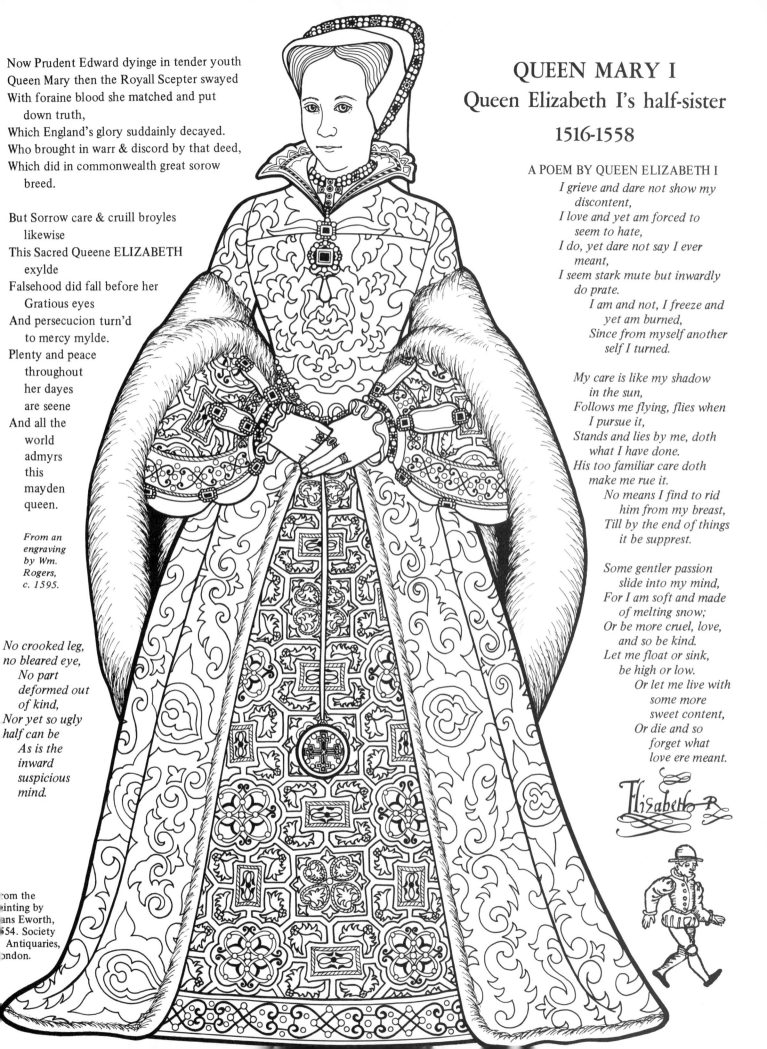

Now Prudent Edward dyinge in tender youth
Queen Mary then the Royall Scepter swayed
With foraine blood she matched and put
    down truth,
Which England's glory suddainly decayed.
Who brought in warr & discord by that deed,
Which did in commonwealth great sorow
    breed.

But Sorrow care & cruill broyles
    likewise
This Sacred Queene ELIZABETH
    exylde
Falsehood did fall before her
    Gratious eyes
And persecucion turn'd
    to mercy mylde.
Plenty and peace
    throughout
    her dayes
    are seene
And all the
    world
    admyrs
    this
    mayden
    queen.

*From an
engraving
by Wm.
Rogers,
c. 1595.*

*No crooked leg,
no bleared eye,
No part
deformed out
    of kind,
Nor yet so ugly
half can be
    As is the
    inward
    suspicious
    mind.*

From the
inting by
ans Eworth,
554. Society
Antiquaries,
ondon.

QUEEN MARY I
Queen Elizabeth I's half-sister
1516-1558

A POEM BY QUEEN ELIZABETH I

*I grieve and dare not show my
    discontent,
I love and yet am forced to
    seem to hate,
I do, yet dare not say I ever
    meant,
I seem stark mute but inwardly
    do prate.
    I am and not, I freeze and
        yet am burned,
    Since from myself another
        self I turned.*

*My care is like my shadow
    in the sun,
Follows me flying, flies when
    I pursue it,
Stands and lies by me, doth
    what I have done.
His too familiar care doth
    make me rue it.
    No means I find to rid
        him from my breast,
    Till by the end of things
        it be supprest.*

*Some gentler passion
    slide into my mind,
For I am soft and made
    of melting snow;
Or be more cruel, love,
    and so be kind.
Let me float or sink,
    be high or low.
    Or let me live with
        some more
        sweet content,
    Or die and so
        forget what
        love ere meant.*

Elisabeth R

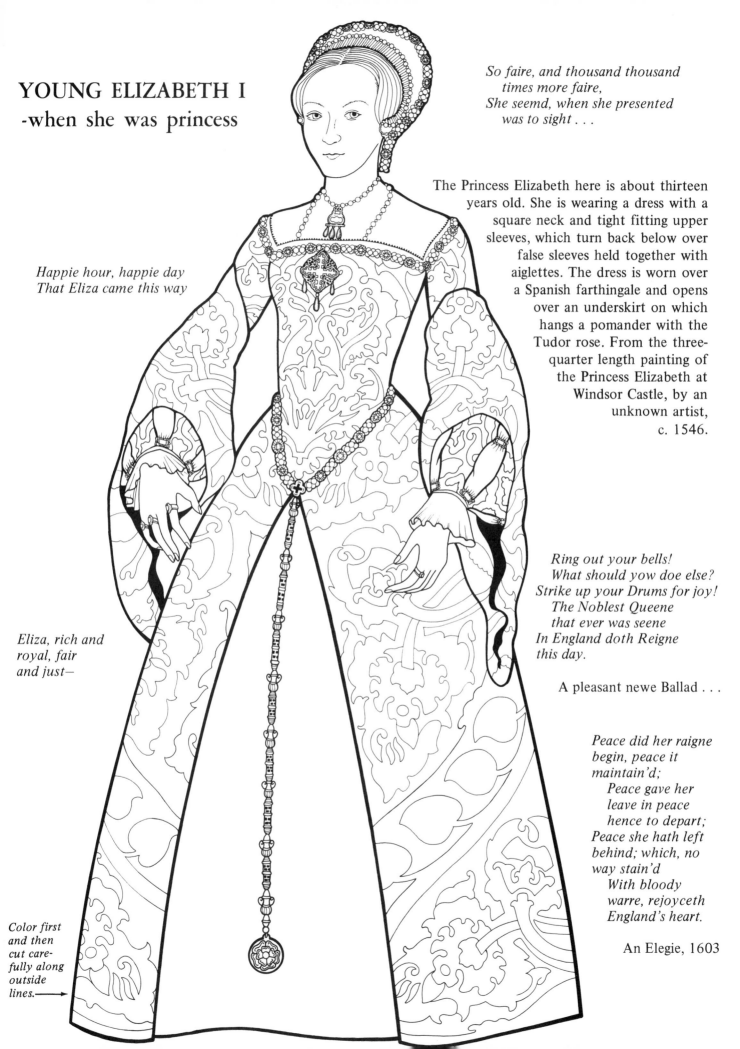

YOUNG ELIZABETH I
-when she was princess

*So faire, and thousand thousand
times more faire,
She seemd, when she presented
was to sight . . .*

The Princess Elizabeth here is about thirteen years old. She is wearing a dress with a square neck and tight fitting upper sleeves, which turn back below over false sleeves held together with aiglettes. The dress is worn over a Spanish farthingale and opens over an underskirt on which hangs a pomander with the Tudor rose. From the three-quarter length painting of the Princess Elizabeth at Windsor Castle, by an unknown artist, c. 1546.

*Happie hour, happie day
That Eliza came this way*

*Eliza, rich and
royal, fair
and just—*

*Ring out your bells!
What should yow doe else?
Strike up your Drums for joy!
The Noblest Queene
that ever was seene
In England doth Reigne
this day.*

A pleasant newe Ballad . . .

*Peace did her raigne
begin, peace it
maintain'd;
Peace gave her
leave in peace
hence to depart;
Peace she hath left
behind; which, no
way stain'd
With bloody
warre, rejoyceth
England's heart.*

An Elegie, 1603

Color first
and then
cut care-
fully along
outside
lines.→

MARY QUEEN OF SCOTS

—that miserable accident, far contrary to my meaning. How innocent I am in this case.

Elizabeth to James of Scotland about the execution of his mother, Mary Queen of Scots. February 14, 1587. British Museum, Cotton MS CIX.

Mary Stuart is 16 years old in this picture. She is wearing balloon puffs on her shoulders which are ornamented with gold cords held together with pearls. Her tiny waist was moulded by a steel corset.

The Daughter of Debate
That eke discord doth sow,
Shall reap no gain where former rule
Hath taught still peace to grow.

From the drawing by Francois Clouet in the Musée Condé, Chantilly, and the engraving by Hans Huys, 1559.

QUEEN ELIZABETH I WEARING THE PHOENIX

In this most famous and peerlesse governement of her most excellent Majesty, her subjects through the speciall assistance, and blessing of God, in searching the most opposite corners and quarters of the world, and to speake plainly, in compassing the vaste globe of the earth more than once, have excelled all the nations and people of the earth. For, which of the kings of this land before her Majesty, had theyr banners ever seene in the Caspian sea? which of them hath ever dealt with the Emperor of Persia, as her Majesty hath done, and obtteined for her merchants large & loving privileges? who ever saw before this regiment, an English Ligier in the stately porch of the Grand Signor at Constantinople? who ever found English Consuls & Agents at Tripolis in Syria, at Aleppo, at Babylon, at Balsara, and which is more, who ever heard of Englishman at Goa before now? what English shippes did heeretofore ever anker in the mighty river of Plate? passe and repasse the unpassable (in former opinion) straight of Magellan, range along the coast of Chile, Peru, and all the backside of Nova Hispania, further then any Christian ever passed, travers the mighty bredth of the South sea, land upon the Luzones in despight of the enemy, enter into alliance, amity, and traffike with the princes of the Moluccaes, & the Isle of Java, double the famous Cape of Bona Seranza, arrive at the Isle of Santa Helena, & last of al returne home most richly laden with the commodities of China, as the subjects of this now flourishing monarchy have gone?

Hakluyt

From the painting by Nicolas Hilliard c. 1575-80, in the National Portrait Gallery (no. 190), London.

Look closely and you can see the phoenix on her breast, rising from the flames. This is the dress on the back cover.

Division kindled Stryfe, Blest Union quenched the flame: Thence sprang our noble Phoenix dear, The peerless Prince of Fame.

Poem from the Norwich Gates, 1578.

For my part, I doubt no whit but that all this tyrannical, proud and brainsick attempt will be the beginning, though not the end, of the ruin of that King (Philip of Spain), that, most unkingly, even in the midst of treating peace, begins this wrongful war.

ELIZABETH TRIUMPHANT

You all pray so heartily for me, as I fear you will by your prayers make me live too long.

He hath procured my greatest glory that meant my sorest wrack, and hath so dimmed the light of his sunshine, that who hath a will to obtain shame, let them keep his forces company.

Elizabeth to James of Scotland, August, 1588. Ryder MS.

From the engraving *Eliza Triumphans* by William Rogers to commemorate the defeat of the Spanish Armada, 1588.

Color first and then cut carefully along outside lines. →

QUEEN ELIZABETH I
The Walsingham Dress

From the painting at Sudeley Castle of Elizabeth I in the Family of Henry VIII, formerly attributed to Hans Eworth, c. 1570.

Sir Francis Walsingham was the principal secretary to Queen Elizabeth I, and the famous painting from which this dress is taken was given to the knight in appreciation by the queen.

*Eliza is the fairest Queene
That ever trod upon this greene.
Eliza's eyes are blessed starres,
Inducing peace, subduing warres.*

Ballad, 1591

*In the widest ocean she her throne does reare,
That over all the earth it may be seene.*

—Faerie Queene

*Elizabeth the English Queene,
The like of whome was never seene.*

Color first and then cut carefully along outside lines. ➞

SIR WALTER RALEIGH
1552? - 1618

*His song was all a
lamentable lay,
Of great unkindnesse,
and of usage hard,
Of Cynthia, the Ladie
of the Sea.*

*Ah! my loves queene, and
goddesse of my life,
Who shall me pittie, when
thou doest me wrong?*

**STANDS FOR
HOLDING UP
THE DOLLS**

**Make a small slit for
the sword in the
hanger on the
knight's side.**

Sir *W. R.* was a tall handsome
man: but he was damnable
proud. In his youth his
Companions were boysterous
blades, but generally those
that had wit. He was no
Slug; without doubt
he had a wonderful
waking spirit.

Aubrey

Sir *W. R.* was the
Summer's Nightingale!

STANDS FOR
HOLDING
THE DOLLS

Robert Devereux
**THE EARL
OF ESSEX**
1566-1601

Who, I fear Raleigh?

*Ah if I might
But gain her
sight.*

*O then should
I Contented
dye.*

From the miniature by
Nicholas Hilliard,
c. 1595;
the Lady Lucas,
London.

*The Queen says he
hath played long
enough upon her,
and that she means
to play awhile
upon him.*

Chamberlain
about Essex

*My lord of Essex
hath chased Mr.
Raleigh from the
court.*

—Sir Fr. Allen to
Anthony Bacon,
1589

—*the general of
our gracious
empress from
Ireland coming,
bringing rebellion
broached on his
sword.*

Henry V, act 5

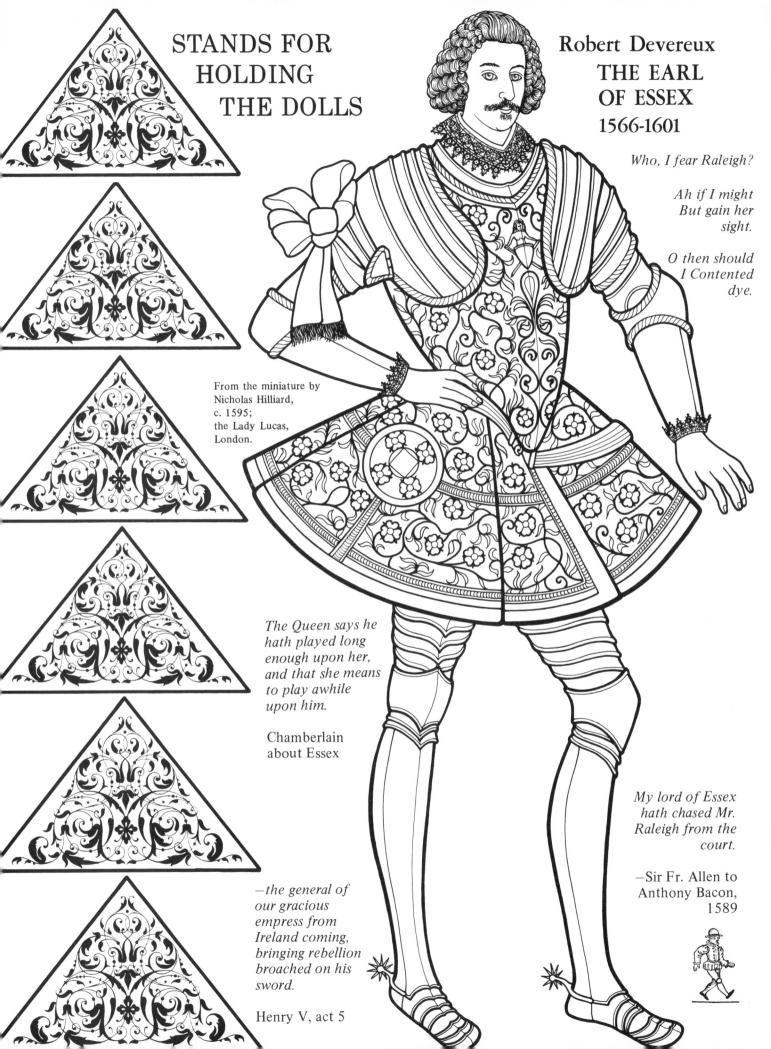

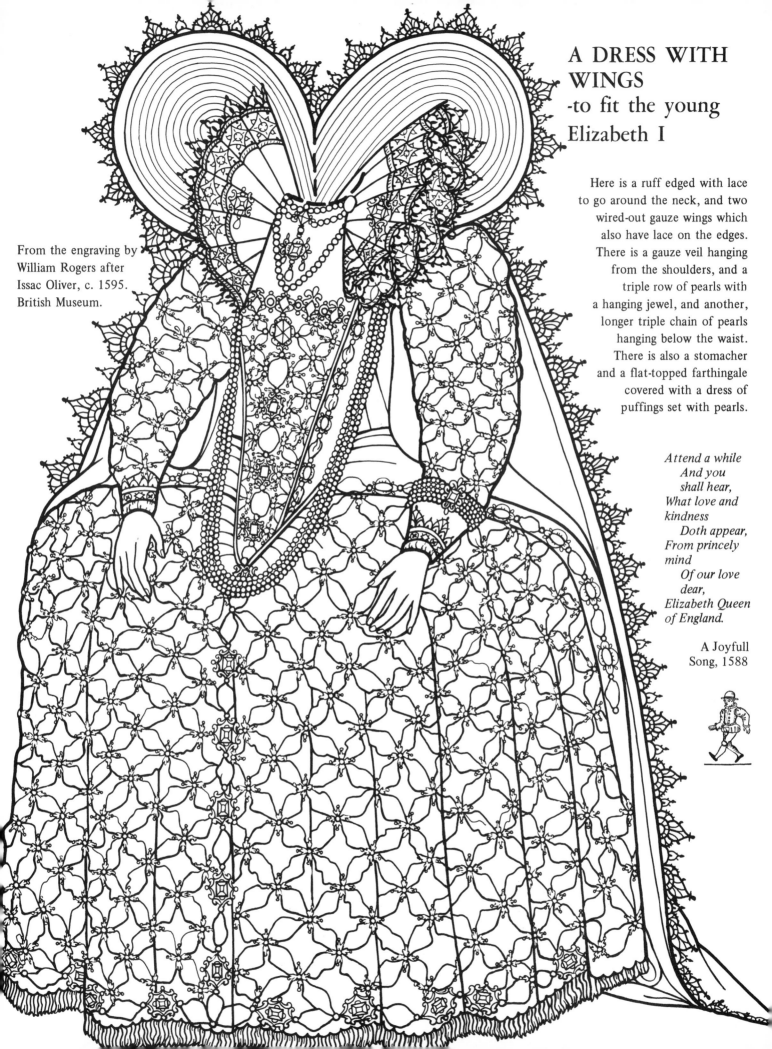

A DRESS WITH WINGS
-to fit the young Elizabeth I

From the engraving by William Rogers after Issac Oliver, c. 1595. British Museum.

Here is a ruff edged with lace to go around the neck, and two wired-out gauze wings which also have lace on the edges. There is a gauze veil hanging from the shoulders, and a triple row of pearls with a hanging jewel, and another, longer triple chain of pearls hanging below the waist. There is also a stomacher and a flat-topped farthingale covered with a dress of puffings set with pearls.

*Attend a while
And you
    shall hear,
What love and
    kindness
        Doth appear,
From princely
    mind
        Of our love
            dear,
Elizabeth Queen
of England.*

A Joyfull
Song, 1588

AN EMBROIDERED DRESS FOR ELIZABETH I

-to fit over the Phoenix dress

Here is a large, circular ruff to cover the neck, and a dress with a band in front of gold embroidery, pearls and jewels in gold mounts. The bodice is festooned with pearls, and the sleeves are embroidered with flowers adorned with jewels. From the painting of Elizabeth I by John Bettes the Younger, c. 1585-90. National Maritime Museum, Greenwich.

The ruff was brought by Catherine de Medici to France in 1533, and from there it quickly came to England. They have three or foure degrees of minor ruffes, placed by degree, step by step, one beneath another, and all under the Maister devil ruffe; the skyrts, then, of these great ruffes are long and side every way, pleated and crested ful curiously, God wot. Then last of all they are either clogged with golde, silver, or silk lace of stately price, wrought all over with needle woork, speckled and sparkled here and there with the sonne, the moone, the stares, and many other antiquities straunge to beholde. Some are wrought with open woork down to the midst of of the ruffe and further, some with close woork some with purled lace so cloyd, and other gewgawes.

Philip Stubbes, 1583.

—while ELIZA raignes
One England *need not fear an hundred* Spains.

Fitzgeffrey

Now flourish Arts, the Queene of Peace doth raigne Histriomastix, *1589.*

This dress is similar to that on the front cover, painted about 1588 to celebrate the defeat of the Spanish Armada. After George Gower, the Serjeant Painter. Trinity College, Cambridge.

This Virgin-Queene did rule faire Albion *Twice two & twenty yeares, with great increase Of peace, joy, wealth, much honour & reknowne . . .*

Sure Her Majesty is made of the same stuff of which the ancients believed the heroes to be formed; that is, her mind of gold, her body of brass.

Essex, 1597.

THE DARNLEY DRESS
-to fit young Elizabeth I

This dress, with a close-fitting bodice, fits over a Spanish farthingale. From the painting by an unknown artist of Elizabeth I formerly belonging to the Earl of Darnley, now in the National Portrait Gallery (no. 2082), London. c. 1575.

On the Queen's coming to Bristol, 1574.

*No sooner was pronounst
    her name,
But babes in street gan leap;
The youth, the age, the rich,
    the poor,
Came running all on heap,
And, clapping hands, cried
    maynly out,
"O blessed be the hour!
Our Queen is coming to the
    Town,
With princely trayn and
    power."*

*Kiss the steps
    Where she doth tred,
That keeps her country
thus.
    In peace and rest,
    And perfect stay;
    In Peace, by
        Peace,
    Our Peace preserve,
        And her long
        life
    Encrease.*

*Now read aright,
    and do not miss,
What jolly dame
    this lady is.*

A DRESS FOR QUEEN MARY I

From the three similar paintings of Queen Mary I by Antonio Mor, c. 1554, in the Prado, Madrid, Castle Ashby, and the Isabella, Stewart Gardner Museum, Boston.

On the front of this dress hangs a great diamond, sent to Queen Mary by Philip of Spain, together with a 'fine pearl' — since called La Pelegrina or the Wanderer, which was brought to Europe by Balboa in 1513. When Queen Mary died, the pearl was returned to Spain and was worn by all the Spanish queens until 1808, when Napoleon took Spain.

From a gold rial of Queen Mary I, 1553.

Such imps of Satan's kind
Do stand and flourish still,
Which do suppress all truth
And do maintain all evil.

Ballad, 1564

Joseph, Napoleon's brother, fled with La Pelegrina, and from him it descended to Louis Napoleon, later Napoleon III, who sold it while in exile in England to the Marquess of Albercorn. The great pearl was very heavy and easily fell out of its holder, and was twice lost, and recovered.

A SPANISH COAT OF FUR AND DAMASK FOR QUEEN ELIZABETH I

-to fit over the Walsingham dress

Fairer and nobler liveth none this hour,
Nor like in grace, nor like in learned
*   skill;*
Therefore they Glorian call
*   that glorious flower:*
Long mayst thou, Glorian,
*   live, in glory and great*
*   power.*

—Faerie Queene

From an engraving
of Elizabeth I
by Hans Huys,
1559.

Ye wonder how this
noble Damozell
So great perfections
did in her compile

God save our Queene,
and God her
Realme defend,
Confound her foes,
and thus I make
an end.

from a young
wyt, 1577

Color first and then cut
carefully along outside lines. →

Sir Francis Drake
1540 - 1590

So Drake (divine Eliza's champion),
    Seizing upon a prey of Indian gold,
Meaning to ship it home to Albion,
    Ballasts his bark with treasures manifold—
    Which when the griev'd Iberians do behold,
They swarm in troops to take his prize away
And to disrob him of his gainèd prey.

A thousand hell-mouth'd cannons' deadly shot,
    A thousand rattling muskets' hail-stones fly,
Yet thousand deadly cannons hurt him not,
    Nor thousand rattling muskets reck'neth he,
    But still rebeats them all as eagerly—
And maugre all their beards brings home the
        spoil,
Riching Eliza and Eliza's soil.

        by *Charles Fitzgeffrey*, 1596

They pictured Sir *Francis Drake*
generally half a Man, half a Dragon.

*From an engraving by
Jodocus Hondius, 1580.*

*We hear that sir Francis Drake is a fearfull man to the Spanish king, and that
the king could have been content that sir Francis had taken last years flete,
so as he had not gone forward to his Indies. We hear that he hath taken seven
rych shippes on the coast of the Indyes. I wish they war saf in the Thames.*

Letter of Lord Burghley to the Earl of Leicester,
March 31, 1586. British Museum Cotton MS. Galba C. IX, f. 149.

The Trouble With the Earl of Essex

by Queen Elizabeth I

(The earl went with a large army to Ireland to deal with the earl of Tyrone, "the capital traitor". But Essex bungled badly.)

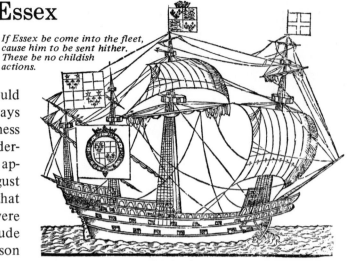

If Essex be come into the fleet, cause him to be sent hither. These be no childish actions.

You have possessed us with expectation that you would proceed as we have directed you, but your actions always show the contrary. To so perform the Ulster wars, if sickness of the army be the reason, why was not the action undertaken when the army was in better state? If winter's approach, why were the summer months of July and August lost? If the spring were too soon, and the summer that followed otherwise spent, if the harvest that succeeded were so neglected as nothing hath been done, we must conclude that none of the four quarters of the year will be in season for you. Further we require you to consider whether we have not a great cause to think that your purpose is not to end the war. The state of every province of Ireland you describe to be in worse conditions than ever they were before you put foot in that kingdom.

Elizabeth R   Letter of September 14, 1599.

He carried into Ireland a heart corrupted, for being a man by nature of high imagination, he was confident that if he had got the flower of the English forces into his hands, and if he might have also the rebels of Ireland, he should be able to ascend to his desired greatness in England. He was resolved to dally out the season, and so to work a mutual obligation between Tyrone and himself. Tyrone returned a message, *That if the Earl of Essex would follow Tyrone's plot, he would make the Earl of Essex the greatest man that ever was in England.*   Francis Bacon

Yea, the late earl of Essex told queen Elizabeth, that her conditions were as crooked as her carcass; but it cost him his head, which his insurrection had not cost him but for that speech.   Sir W. Raleigh, *The Prerogative of Parliaments*

Fame

The Earl in all his journeys did nothing but make circles of errors.

THE TRIUMPH OF QUEEN ELIZABETH I From a drawing by William Teshe after a woodcut, 1594. British Museum, Sloane MS. 1832, f. 7v.

King James I of England and VI of Scotland, and His Queen, Anne of Denmark

—the successor of Queen Elizabeth I
—son of the unfortunate Mary Queen of Scots
and father of the unfortunate
Charles I.

*He would never change
his clothes till very
ragges, and he
never washt his
hands. He had
a very brave
Queen.*

A. Weldon,
1650

*He lived in peace, and left all his Kingdoms in a
peaceable condition. For he had rather spend
100,000 pounds to keep or procure peace
with dishonour, than 10,000 pounds
on an Army that would have
forced peace with honour.*

A. Weldon, 1650

From the engraving by
Renold Elstrack, c. 1603.

The Patrone of
true Holinesse
Foule Errour
doth defeate:
Hypocrisie,
him to entrappe,
Doth to his
home entreate.

Here is Queen Elizabeth I in the role of St. George, vanquishing the Hydra, after T. Cecill, c. 1625.